The Variations Of Strong Love And The Motivation That Drives You To Keep Going

The Variations Of Strong Love And The Motivation That Drives You To Keep Going

Raekwon Williams

Copyright © 2020 by Raekwon Williams.

ISBN-978-1-6455-0865-6

All rights reserved. No part of this book may be reproduced or transmitted in any form or by any means, electronic or mechanical, including photocopying, recording, or by any information storage and retrieval system, without permission in writing from the copyright owner.

The views expressed in this work are solely those of the author and do not necessarily reflect the views of the publisher, and the publisher hereby disclaims any responsibility for them.

Matchstick Literary
1-888-306-8885
orders@matchliterary.com

I would like to dedicate this book to my Grandmother, Ms. Kathy, Grandfather Garry, my sister Nyla, my parents, and friends. Their support really helped me come a long way in my poetry, and after an 11-year journal of writing stories or poems it's finally paid off.

When you love something very deeply it's hard for anything to break you away from it, even if it's the worst thing that you've ever experienced. No matter what happens you keep that love, and you hold it in a special place in your heart that not a single person can understand of you. It holds a side within you that nobody else can understands except you and the thing that you love; it lifts your sprit more than anything else ever will and brings a sense of happiness in your life at the same time. Love in general is powerful, and it changes your perspective of life. It makes you see things from the inside out like never as if you live in a world beyond your imagination. On the other hand, ignoring what haters may think of you is important because you gain more respect when you overachieve by proving them wrong and keeping a positive outlook on things. No matter what someone thinks of you, you can overcome it, and you can't let how someone views your appearance stop you from loving yourself. You should never have to change for anyone and always remember that you've a natural beauty and that beauty is the character that you present yourself as both in the inside and out. The lesson in the following poems is that love is a powerful tool and when you love something deeply you won't ever stop it despite the odds. In connection with that the final lesson is that when you've the right amount of love for yourself and spread yourself with positive energy. Nobody can tell you anything because you control your own faith, you've your own natural beauty and you can overcome negativity with a positive mind.

My Eternal Love For Wrestling

𝕴t is the sport that broke me apart from my mother's wombs at birth.

It is the sport that had me rocking back and forth in my crib, just as my dad had it turned on right near my tiny little eyes, when I was just a baby.

The older I grew, the more loving it became, and I grew to love the sport more and more at every step that I aged.

Wrestling is my love, my eternal love, it is a sport that I will cherish with me now until my death.

Nothing can take me away from my love, not a sound of negativity can do the trick, not a sound of thunder can take this away.

Not a pound of raindrops can fully erase my love from me, not a death of a loved one can bring us apart.

𝒮urely, I will shed a tear, and feel extremely hurt when losing my family members. But as touching as that maybe my love for wrestling remains eternal.

It beats within my soul every time I open my eyes, it beats within my heart, no matter if I'm sad or happy.

𝔑othing understands me like wrestling understands me, everyday I've to watch my love, and even on my worst days wrestling is there for me.

Never once has my love let me down, it's always been there thru the goods, the bad, the struggle, and the fight.

My love explodes my energy every time I watch it, my love turns my mood around, and it makes me simile even when I don't want to.

It is a strong love, it is an eternal love, wrestling is my life, and can't nobody tell me otherwise.

When I'm In Love

Ain't nothing better than the sweet feeling of being in love
When I'm in love, it makes my fingers tangle, like the feathers from a bird's wings.
When I'm in love, closed doors become opened

When I'm in love, loud mouths become soft
When I'm in love, winter becomes the spring

When I'm in love, cold water becomes warm
When I'm in love, school feels less cruel

When I'm in love, poor people seem rich
When I'm in love, food taste healthier and less fattening

When I'm in love, babies can walk before the age of 2
When I'm in love, people speak more generous

When I'm in love, trains wait for people to come in
When I'm in love, trees don't fall on houses

When I'm in love, natural disasters are nonexistence
When I'm in love, movies feel more creative and less descriptive

When I'm in love, music sounds more clean
When I'm in love, fighters become lovers

When I'm in love, enemies become friends
When I'm in love, fantasies become real

When I'm in love, it feels like a utopia
When I'm in love, it feels like a whole new world

Positive Thinkers Overcome

They say you can't sing, you sing louder
They say you can't dance, you dance at a frequency

They say you can't read, you grab 16 books
They say you can't write, you grab 20 sheets of paper

They say your not creative, you draw a whole house
They say you can't cook, you cook a whole dinner

They say you score average on test; you start scoring above it
They say you can't drive, you better push that gas pedal as hard as you can

They say you can't ride a bike, you push the pedals faster
They say your not smart, you expose them with knowledge

They say your lonely, you make friends with 10 random people
They say your afraid of bugs, you step on a cock roach

They say your afraid of the dark, you go in a room with no lights
They say your not a risk taker, you get on the first airplane that you see

No matter what they say, positive thinkers will overcome
Positive thinkers embrace the hate

Positive thinkers turn hate to love
Positive thinkers turn bad words into good ones

Positive thinkers turn rain into the sun
Positive thinkers turn darkness to light

Positive thinkers don't let anything hurt them
Positive thinkers overcome anything that stands in their way

Be Proud of Who You Are

You are as pretty as the stars that glow at night
You may not realize your beauty, but that's alright

You probably think that your ugly, but that's a shame
The people who do think that your ugly are really lame

Can't nobody shame you of your looks
Those people who do shame you are just crooks

You maybe short, but so what
You better be the happiest short person in the world

You maybe to tall, but does it really matter?
You should be happy with your height, and embrace it

You maybe fat, but don't let the haters talk you down
Just take care of yourself, and let the haters keep chirping

Be proud of who you are, no one should've to change for nobody
Be proud of who you are, if your short be damn proud of it

Be proud of who you are, can't nobody tell you that you ain't beautiful
Be proud of who you are, dress the same way as you normally do

Be proud of who you are, if you're a nerd then
enlighten people with your brilliance
Be proud of who you are, if you like to dance then
don't be afraid to be the first person on the dance floor

Be proud of who you are, if you like to sing, then spread your voice with joy like the hummingbirds when the sun arises in the morning.

𝔅e proud of who you are, don't let your weight conflict you, be confident with it, nobody should be telling you to lose or gain that's your choice

Be proud of who you are because in the end you've control over your own destiny